Cranbury Public Library

23 North Main St., Cranbury, NJ 08512
(609) 655-055   ?09) 655-2858

www.Cranb

D1539774

Ice Cream

by **Dana Meachen Rau**

Reading Consultant: Nanci R. Vargus, Ed.D.

Marshall Cavendish
Benchmark
New York

Picture Words

 bowl

 cherry

 cone

 ice cream

 ice cream truck

 pie

 sundaes

in a bar.

on a stick.

The is melting!

So hurry and lick!

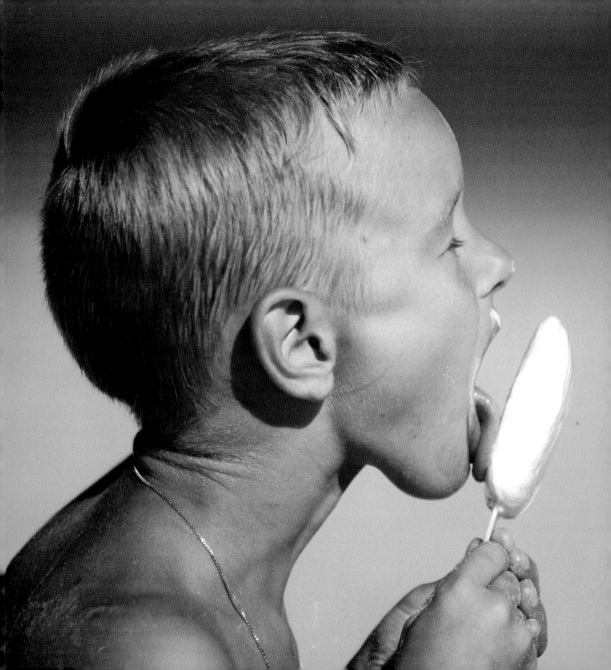

is good on top

of .

We wave when the goes by.

 on a .

Do not let it drop!

 in a  with a  on top!

We make  we can eat.

Sharing is very sweet!

Words to Know

cone (kohn)
    a holder for ice cream that you
    can eat

hurry (HUR-ee)
    to move fast

melting to turn watery

sundae (SUN-day)
    ice cream with lots of toppings

Find Out More

Books

Gibbons, Gail. *Ice Cream: The Full Scoop*. New York: Holiday House, 2006.

Greenstein, Elaine. *Ice-cream Cones for Sale!* New York: Arthur A. Levine Books, 2003.

Thoennes Keller, Kristin. *From Milk to Ice Cream*. Mankato, MN: Capstone Press, 2004.

Videos

Madden, Scott. *Field Trip: Ice Cream*. Ponte Vedra Beach, FL: MediaPro.

Vermont Story Works. *Let's Go to the Ice Cream and Yogurt Factory*. Burlington, VT: Vermont Story Works.

Web Sites

Ben and Jerry's
www.benjerry.com

PBS Kids: ZOOM: Homemade Ice Cream
pbskids.org/zoom/activities/cafe/homemade icecream.html

USDA: MyPyramid.gov
www.mypyramid.gov/kids/index.html

About the Author

Dana Meachen Rau is an author, editor, and illustrator. A graduate of Trinity College in Hartford, Connecticut, she has written more than two hundred books for children, including nonfiction, biographies, early readers, and historical fiction. She likes to eat ice cream with her family in Burlington, Connecticut.

About the Reading Consultant

Nanci R. Vargus, Ed.D., wants all children to enjoy reading. She used to teach first grade. Now she works at the University of Indianapolis. Nanci helps young people become teachers. She wishes ice cream could be a meal!

Marshall Cavendish Benchmark
99 White Plains Road
Tarrytown, NY 10591-5502
www.marshallcavendish.us

All Internet addresses were correct at the time of printing.

Library of Congress Cataloging-in-Publication Data

Rau, Dana Meachen, 1971–
Ice cream / by Dana Meachen Rau.
    p. cm. — (Benchmark Rebus : What's Cooking?)
Summary: "Easy to read text with rebuses explores the different ways to enjoy ice cream"—Provided by publisher.
Includes bibliographical references.
ISBN 978-0-7614-2893-0
1. Ice cream, ices, etc.—Juvenile literature. I. Title.
TX795.R39 2008
641.8'62—dc22
        2007022340

Editor: Christine Florie
Publisher: Michelle Bisson
Art Director: Anahid Hamparian
Series Designer: Virginia Pope

Photo research by Connie Gardner

Rebus images, with the exception of ice cream truck and sundaes, provided courtesy of *Dorling Kindersley*.

Cover photo by Banana Stock/Alamy

The photographs in this book are used with the permission and through the courtesy of:
AP Photo/The Plain Dealer, Lynn Ischay, p. 3 (ice cream truck); AP Photo/Jupiter Images, p. 3 (sundae);
PhotoEdit: pp. 5, 19 David Young Wolff; *Jupiter Images*: p. 7 Burke/Triolo Productions, p. 11 Matt Bowman/Food Pix;
Corbis: p. 9 Torleif Svenson; p. 17 J. Barry O'Rourke; p. 21 Tom Stewart; *Getty Images*: p. 13 Ariel Skelley;
p. 15 Joe Major/DK Stock.

Printed in Malaysia
1 3 5 6 4 2